Tudor & Stuart Times

TONY D. TRIGGS

This book is dedicated to my daughter, Donna

ACKNOWLEDGEMENTS

The author and publishers would like to thank the following for permission to reproduce photographs and other material:

Bodleian Library, Oxford	11; 43; 49; 52
The Bridgeman Art Library Ltd. and	
The Royal College of Physicians, London	54
By permission of The British Library	cover; 10
Cadw: Welsh Historic Monuments (Crown Copyright)	39
Donald Cooper	42
Edinburgh University Library	30
The English Civil War Society	45
English Heritage	12; 18; 24; 33
Historic Royal Palaces (Crown Copyright)	24-25
The Hulton Picture Library	37
Kentwell Hall	5
Leicestershire Museums, Arts and Records Services	11
The Master and Fellows, Magdalene College, Cambridge	cover; 50; 51
Mansell Collection	16; 17; 54
By kind permission of the Marquess of Tavistock	
and the Trustees of the Bedford Estates	34
Mary Evans Picture Library	cover; 20; 21; 23; 33; 40; 41; 45; 46 (Explorer); 47
Mary Rose Trust, Portsmouth	28
National Maritime Museum Publications	cover; 35; 36
By courtesy of The National Portrait Gallery, London	20; 21; 23; 41
The National Trust	25; 32 (Mike Cadwell)
Reproduced from the (1992) Ordnance Survey 1:25 000	
map with the permission of the Controller of H.M.S.O. ©	10
David Parker/Science Photo Library	55
Rex Features (Photographers) Ltd.	53
Shakespeare Centre Library: Thos. F. and Mig Holte Collection	33
Ronald Sheridan/Ancient Art and Architecture Collection	cover; title; 9; 16-19; 20; 21; 24; 27-31; 38; 39; 45; 47; 53; 55
Suffolk Record Office (Ipswich)	8
Thomas-Photos, Oxford	42
Tony D. Triggs	13; 25
Westminster Cathedral and Weidenfeld & Nicolson Archives	cover; 27
Windsor Castle, Royal Library © 1992 Her Majesty The Queen	26

First published 1992 by Folens Limited, Dunstable and Dublin.
Folens Limited, Albert House, Apex Business Centre, Boscombe Road, Dunstable LU5 4RL, England.

ISBN 1 85276178-4

Cover Design: Hybert Design & Type
Illustrators: Peter Dennis of Linda Rogers Associates
Paul Nicholls
Printed in Singapore by Craft Print.

CONTENTS

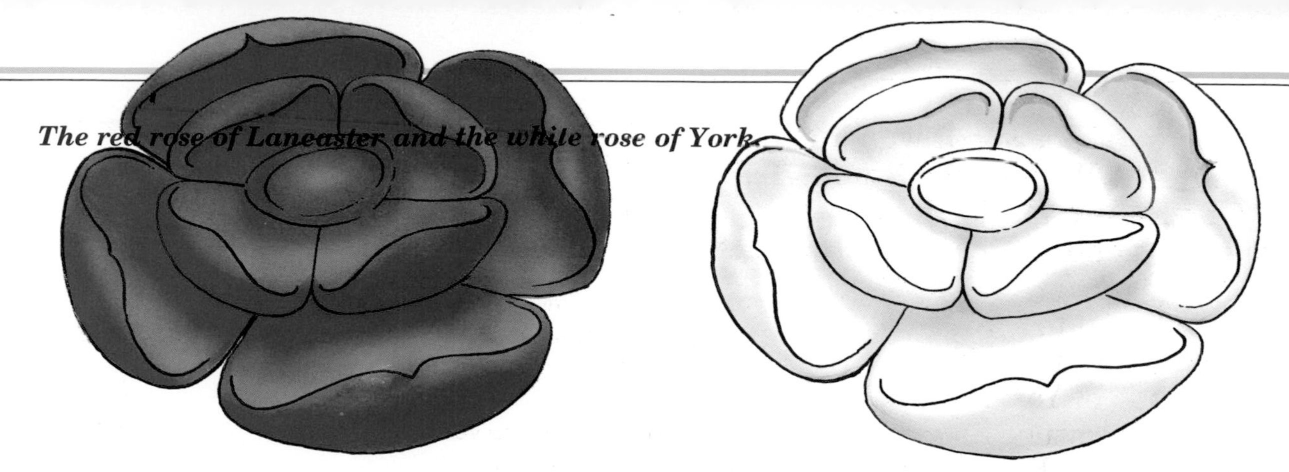

The red rose of Lancaster and the white rose of York.

Stripped of its armour and clothing, torn by wounds and covered with mud, the dead king's body was thrown on to an old horse ...

1. Tudor and Stuart Kings and Queens

The words in yellow were written just after the Battle of Bosworth in 1485. The dead king was Richard III; the winner of the Battle was a prince called Henry Tudor. Henry Tudor took Richard's place as king of England and Wales. He is usually known as Henry VII.

For 30 years before the Battle there had been gang warfare in England as two branches of the royal family fought for power. One branch was known as the House of Lancaster and the other was known as the House of York. Each side had a rose on its banner or badge, so the wars are called the Wars of the Roses.

Both sides had very powerful supporters. These included the barons - men who owned huge amounts of land. The barons controlled the lives of the men and women who lived on their land, and could order the men to fight on their side. It was hard for a king to destroy the barons who fought against him.

Someone said of Richard III shortly after he died:

He was small of body and weak in strength but he most bravely defended himself as a noble knight to his last breath. He was killed fighting manfully in the thick of his enemies.

Richard III.
What sort of man?

Look again at the things that were written about Richard shortly after he died.

1. Do you think the writers liked him or not?
2. Whose soldiers took his body from the battlefield? Why do you think so?

The Battle of Bosworth was the last battle in the Wars of the Roses. The new king, Henry VII, brought the Wars to an end. Here are some clues about Henry VII's character:

- He belonged to the House of Lancaster but he chose a wife from the House of York.
- When he captured a youth pretending to be a rival prince, he spared his life and gave him a job in his kitchens.

The roses

Look at the rose designs used by the House of Lancaster and the House of York. Then look at the Tudor Rose in the photograph.

1. When do you think people started to use the Tudor Rose?
2. Why do you think they invented it?

Henry VII. What sort of man?

Discuss the clues about Henry.

1. What sort of person do you think Henry was?

This mansion (large house) was built by some Tudors. The courtyard has a huge pattern called a Tudor Rose.

Henry VII and his children and grandchildren (known as the Tudors).

Henry VII 1485-1509

Henry VIII 1509-1547

Edward VI 1547-1553

Mary I 1553-1558

Elizabeth I 1558-1603

Elizabeth was the last of the Tudor monarchs (kings and queens). She did not have any children, so when she died the English invited her cousin King James VI of Scotland to be king of England too.

England had not had a King James before, so the English called him James I. James's family name was Stuart, and on this page you can see the Stuart monarchs.

James I of England 1603-1625

Charles I 1625-1646

Charles II 1660-1685

James II 1685-1688

William III and Mary 1689-1702

Queen Anne 1702-1714

(The dates given are the years the kings and queens ruled.)

Hark, hark,
The dogs do bark,
The beggars are coming to town;
Some in rags,
Some in jags
And one in a velvet gown.

2. Life in the Country

A weaver had this house built for himself at Kersey in Suffolk. Do you think he was rich or poor? (Reading this page will help you decide.)

In the 16th century most people lived in villages and they never saw a town in their lives. Their wooden homes were like giant huts. There was just one room in the hut, with a floor of bare earth and a fire in the middle for cooking and warmth.

Roofs were usually thatched with straw. Smoke from the fire escaped through the thatch and through cracks and small windows, which had no glass. Only the rich could afford to have glass.

Cottagers' homes

Read the description on the left, then answer these questions.

1. Villagers sometimes coated their wooden buildings with clay. Why do you think they did this?
2. What danger do you think the cottagers faced when they lit a fire?
3. The cottagers had very little furniture. What do you think they slept on?
4. Apart from their fires, what do you think the cottagers burned to give themselves light?

Nowadays, most of our food comes from shops. There is plenty of it and few people bother to grow their own. In the Tudor and Stuart times, most people had to grow food or they would have starved. They had herbs and vegetables in their gardens and crops and animals in their fields. There might be corn in one field, peas in another and sheep in a third. They used the sheep's wool to make themselves clothes. There was rarely any wool or cloth left over to sell.

Life could be very hard for the villagers. Often the local miller charged too much for grinding their grain into flour. Sometimes he kept some flour for himself, leaving the villagers hungry. They also went hungry whenever bad weather ruined their crops.

Life became even harder when rich people started to keep more sheep. Unlike the cottagers, they could earn money by selling cloth abroad - it was England's main export. They stopped letting poor people use the land - sometimes by raising the rents so high that no one could pay them. They even began to fence in commons (land that people had always shared). The commons, too, became part of the new, gigantic sheep farms.

A weaver and a spinner. What do you think the third worker is doing?

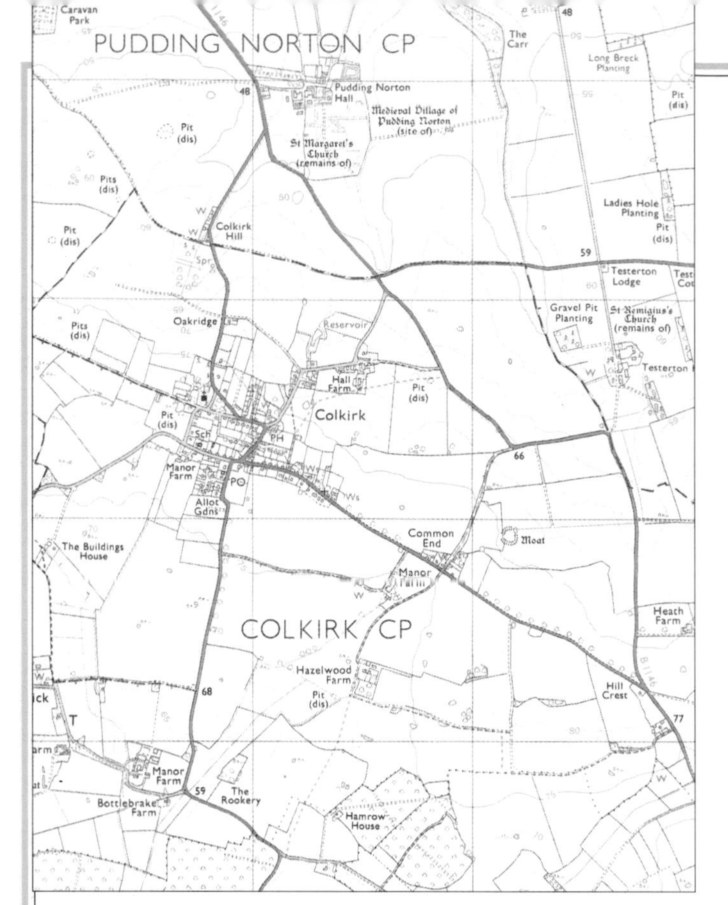

A map of the Colkirk area in Norfolk. Can you see any signs of villages that have disappeared?

One man explained:

Good towns are decayed in their houses, streets and other buildings. Poverty reigns everywhere, and few men can give anything for the repair of highways and bridges.

Sheep are the cause of all these mischiefs. It was far better when there was not only enough sheep, but also oxen, cows, pigs, geese and chickens, eggs, butter and cheese - yes, and bread, corn, and malt besides, and all produced on the same land.

Lately, I have heard of a dozen ploughs - all of them less than six miles from here - abandoned in the last seven years; and where 40 people had their living, now there is just one man and his shepherd.

What happened to all the country folk who had to give up their ploughs and their homes? Many were forced to go begging in towns. Soon the few towns that existed were full of beggars. The citizens felt they were being invaded.

Fencing in land for sheep was called enclosure. It left the poor with less land on which to grow their food, and food was often too expensive to buy.

This is what poor people had to say:

The more sheep, the dearer is the wool.
The more sheep, the dearer is the mutton.
The more sheep, the dearer is the beef.
The more sheep, the dearer is the corn.
The more sheep, the scanter (scarcer) is the white meat (butter and cheese).
The more sheep, the fewer eggs for a penny.

What is this man doing?

When people left Tudor villages the houses fell down but the villages did not always disappear completely. The photograph shows that the tracks and houses sometimes left patterns in the ground. Ploughing has often smoothed them out, but the drawing shows that the pattern can reappear in a field of growing crops. This is because the depth of the soil affects their height.

Enclosure and poverty

Think about the changes in the countryside.

1. "Sheep eat up men." What do you think people meant by this in Tudor times?
2. The rhyme at the start of the chapter is from Tudor times. It tells us the sort of thing that happened but it may not be exactly true. Do you think any beggars might have been seen in posh velvet gowns? Why do you think so?

The hunt for food

Think about the villagers who were going to the towns.

1. Pretend that your family is having to leave its cottage and move to the town in search of food. Discuss how you feel. (There are probably lots of different feelings mixed up inside you.)
   OR
2. Pretend that you live in town and discuss how you feel about country people who come begging or asking for food and work.

A growing town - an early 17th century map of Windsor.

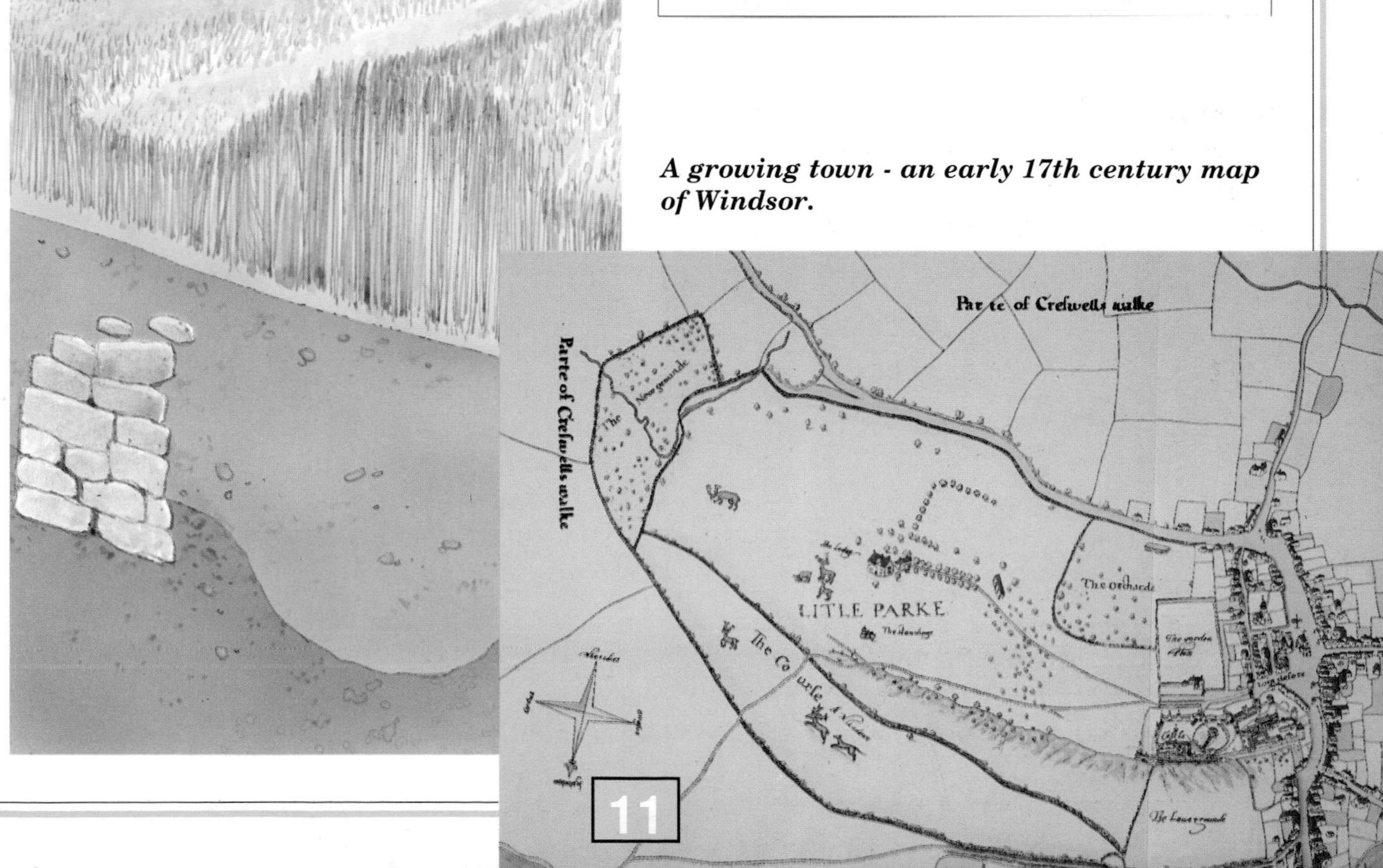

A life of prayer and holiness - strict, harsh and always the same.

A drawing showing parts of a monastery.

3. Life in a Monastery

Monasteries were places where men or women lived, prayed, and obeyed strict rules. They owned more land and employed more workers than anyone else.

What work was done in this room?

Servants lived at monasteries and other workers came from nearby villages to help with jobs like brewing beer, baking bread, cooking meals, shoeing horses and milling grain.

The monks and nuns lived a very hard life. A bell woke them during the night for prayers. There were more prayers at dawn - but nothing to eat.

During the day there were jobs to be done. Older monks or nuns taught the younger ones, or copied out books. After midday prayers they met in a room with hard stone seats, where they had to sit without fidgeting while someone read a chapter from their book of rules. They were then allowed to go for a walk and speak to each other. (This was the only time they could do so.)

Dinner was the only real meal of the day, so they must have been hungry. They ate without talking, but one of the monks or nuns read aloud from the Bible. After a nap they had more prayers, then they studied or worked in the fields until it began to get dark. They ended their day on beds of straw in a chilly dormitory.

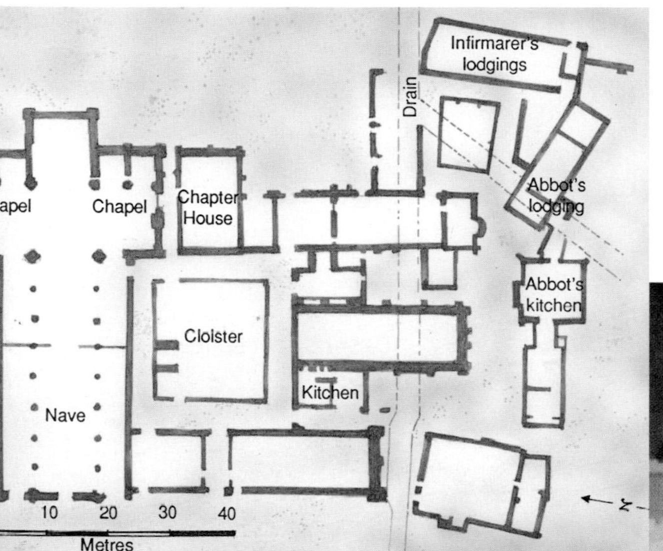

A plan of Roche Abbey in Tudor times.

Roche Abbey

Some monasteries were called abbeys. Look at the plan of Roche Abbey.

1. Who do you think the abbot or abbess was?
2. Find the abbot's lodgings and kitchen. Why do you think the abbot had separate accommodation?
3. Find the Chapter House. This was the place where the monks held their daily meeting. How do you think it got its name?
4. What do you think the warming house was for? Why do you think the monks often had to use it?

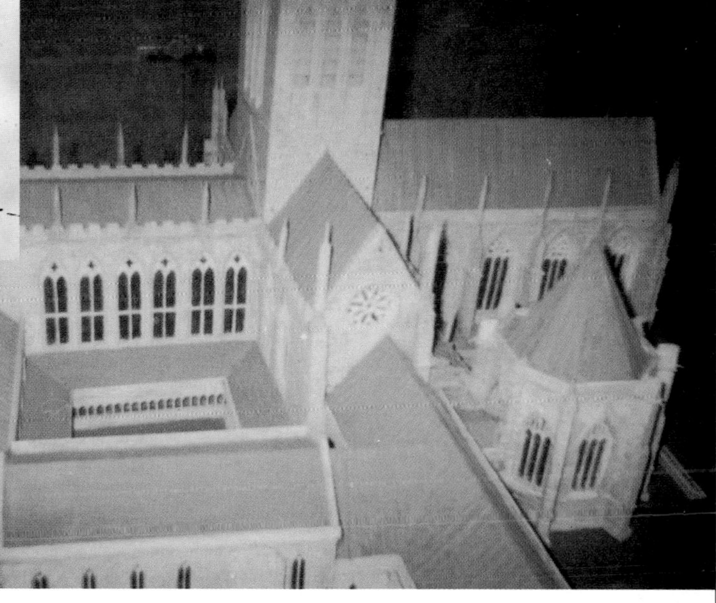

A model of Bolton Priory in Yorkshire, showing how it was before it was ruined.

Monastery life

The poor and the sick went to the monastery for help. Monasteries were the only hospitals in the country.

1. "I was hungry - all I had was the bag of flour they gave me at the monastery."
   Write two other sentences in which people say how the monastery helped them.

A very hard life

Think about the description of a monk's daily life in a monastery.

1. Pretend that you are a monk and write your diary for a week. Monasteries cared for the sick, and you might have been visited by an ill person or someone in need of shelter and food. Perhaps a new worker joined the monastery or bad weather destroyed all the crops.
   Remember to write how you felt when these things happened.

Then suddenly the king's men came, and the monks were turned out.

4. Destroying the Monasteries

In 1536, Henry VIII and his advisers decided to close down the monasteries. They said that the monks and nuns were living evil, sinful and wasteful lives.

Henry VIII's actions affected everyone in the country. He and his friends took the monasteries' farms, but they often used them for sheep, not crops, and many workers lost their jobs.

A man called Michael Sherbrook wrote about the destruction of the monasteries:

It would have upset everyone to see merchants tearing lead from the church roof and hurling it down inside the church, so that all the tombs in the church were broken; they tore up the seats where the monks had sat during services, and they burned them and used them to melt the lead ...

Local farmers and gentlemen bought the timber from the church roof, and others tore the iron supports from the walls. After robbing the church they robbed the abbot's lodgings and all the other buildings . Nothing was left except the cowsheds and the pigsties.

My father bought some wood from the church ... Thirty years later I asked him ... 'Why were you so ready to wreck all the buildings?' 'Why not?' he answered. 'I wanted to have my share of the stuff so I just did what everyone else was doing.'

Closing the monasteries

Look again at the first few lines of this chapter.

1. Discuss Henry's reasons for destroying the monasteries.

Raiding the monasteries

Read what Sherbrook had to say.

1. Do you think he saw what happened or do you think he heard it all from his father?
2. Do you think we can trust his account? Why?

Some people did try to save the monasteries. In northern England an angry mob rose up against Henry led by a man called Robert Aske. In the end Henry's troops defeated the rebels. Aske was captured and sentenced to death.

Destroying a monastery.

Robert Aske wrote about the monasteries just before he died:

Many were in the mountains or moors, where the people are very rough and unruly. These people gained a great deal of good from the monks' teaching and preaching.

No one can stay the night there now. But there was a time when people who needed horsemeat or mansmeat could go to a monastery; and they even helped educated people with money if they got into debt.

Abbeys near the sea kept sea walls and dykes in good condition. They also looked after bridges and roads and did other things for the good of the country.

For the rich or poor?

Read the description given by Aske on the monasteries.

1. Aske mentioned "horsemeat and mansmeat". What might he have meant by this?
2. "Monasteries didn't help the poor - they helped the rich." Do you think Aske would have agreed with this? Why?

Questions from the king's official

Pretend that you are coming back home from a monastery with a laden wagon. You are stopped by one of the king's officials.

1. Write about the meeting. Perhaps the official wants to know what is in your wagon and how you found it. What are you going to do with it all? Act out your scene with a partner.

The printing press - one of the most important inventions ever.

5. New Ideas and Lands

At the start of Henry VIII's reign the Church was very powerful and it tried to control people's thoughts and ideas. It could do this because there were very few books. Good ways of printing were being invented, but books had always been copied by hand in monasteries, and the Church decided which should be copied and which should be burned.

Gutenberg's printing press, about 1460.

Artists like Michelangelo showed the strength and beauty of the human body.

Johann Gutenberg was one of the first printers in Europe.

- The Church taught people to feel ashamed of their lives and their bodies. Some people tried to avoid being punished after their death by giving money and gifts to the Church, and this helped to make it richer than ever.
- The Church said that the sun and the stars go round the earth.
- The Church stuck to old ideas about how the body worked.

The title page to Andreas Versalius' major work on the structure of the human body.

This first chappitre of the first tractate sheweth vn=
der what kyng the playe of the Chesse was founden and
maad. Capitulo primo

Amonge alle the euyl condicions & signes that may
be in a man the first and the grettest is. Whan he fe
reth not ne dredeth to displese & make wroth god by synne
& the peple by lyuyng disordynatly / Whan he retcheth not
nor taketh hede vnto them that repreue hym and his vy/
ces, But sleeth them. In suche wyse as did the emperour
nero. Whiche did do slee his mayster seneque, for as moche
as he myght not suffre to be repreuyd & taught of hym. in
like wise was sõtyme a kyng in babilon that was named

William Caxton was the first English printer. Look at this page from one of his books and see if you can read any of the words.

Suddenly, scholars began to challenge these beliefs. This was partly because new printing presses helped them to share and spread their ideas. Copying out a book by hand could take a year; now hundreds of copies could be printed and sold in a month or two.

- Scientists (like Galileo) proved that the earth goes round the sun.
- Anatomists (like Vesalius) defied the Church and cut up dead bodies to study the organs.
- People soon learned that the world was round (not flat as the Church had always taught) and they heard about newly-discovered continents.

The world was a wonderful place for people who wanted to learn and think for themselves; they were no longer willing to let the Church stop them. Nor were they willing to let the Church rule their everyday lives. The head of the Church was the Pope in Rome. People had felt they belonged to the Church, but now they were starting to feel that they belonged to nations, such as England or France.

The ruins of Roche Abbey.

Henry VIII, who made himself head of the Church in England, being given a book. What do you think the book might be?

Some people thought that the monasteries did a lot of good work; others felt that they helped the Church to rule people's lives, and in Switzerland, Sweden and parts of Germany local rulers closed them down. When Henry VIII closed the monasteries in England he was copying what was happening in much of northern Europe. Local rulers also ended the Pope's control of the Church, and Henry VIII made himself the head of the Church in England.

The Church sometimes killed or bullied people who criticised it, but scholars like Erasmus, Luther and Calvin spoke up bravely. They said that the Church was too rich and greedy, and they spoke out against a lot of the things it was teaching and doing.

Head of the Church

Read about why the monasteries were being closed.

1. Who became head of the Church in England? Whose place did he take?

The map shows all the land that people in Europe knew about up to the time of the Tudors.

Try to pick out Europe, Asia and Africa on this 15th century map.

Explorers thought that if the world was round they could sail west from Europe to get to Asia. Instead, they came to North and South America - whole continents they had never heard of.

Christopher Columbus sailed from Spain in 1492. He was one of the first explorers to reach America. He and the native people must have been very surprised to see each other.

Here are some of the things Columbus wrote about the natives:

I gave some of them red caps, glass beads and many other little things, and they brought us parrots and balls of cotton and spears and many other things.

They would make fine servants, and when I leave I will bring back half a dozen of them. With fifty men we could overcome all the natives and make them do what we wanted. We could take them to Spain or make them slaves on their own land.

Old World meets New World

Look again at Columbus's words.

1. Why do you think the native people did not write anything about Columbus?
2. What do you think people from Europe were planning to do with the natives' land? (Columbus's last few words should give you a very good clue.)
3. Find Europe, America and Asia on a globe of the world. Make sure you can understand the mistake the Explorers made.

Columbus discovers America.

He made up his mind what he wanted - and got it.

6. Henry VIII - in Health and in Sickness

Jane Seymour.

Anne Boleyn.

Henry and his six wives.

Catherine of Aragon.

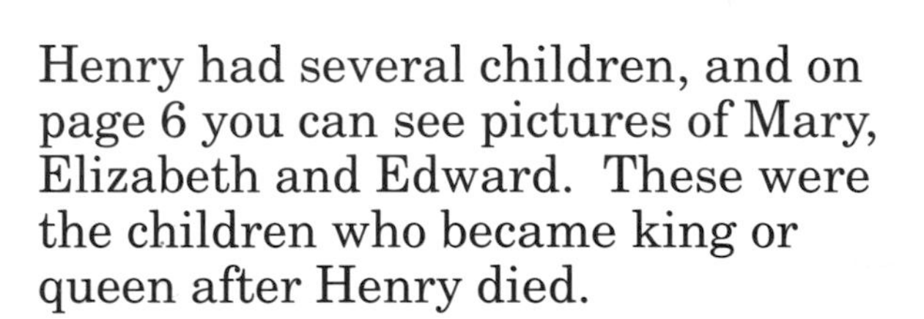

Henry had several children, and on page 6 you can see pictures of Mary, Elizabeth and Edward. These were the children who became king or queen after Henry died.

Mary was the child of Henry and his first wife Catherine of Aragon. The English preferred to be ruled by a king and not by a queen, so Henry wanted a son to take his place when he died. When Catherine got too old to have any more children, Henry divorced her and married a younger woman called Anne Boleyn.

Henry and Anne had a daughter, Elizabeth, but Henry was desperate to have a son. He had Anne beheaded and married for a third time. His new wife, Jane Seymour, died a year later - soon after giving birth to a son, Edward.

Henry married three more times but had no more children. Henry was always afraid that his precious son would die young. In those days most people died of diseases before they grew up.

Henry was keen on music. This picture shows him playing an instrument called a lute.

Anne of Cleves.

Catherine Howard.

Catherine Parr.

Here are some things people said about Henry:

Henry as a teenager:

His majesty is the handsomest prince I ever set eyes on; taller than usual and with very fine legs. His skin is light and glowing and he has reddish brown hair which is straight and short in the French style. His chubby face is so beautiful that it would suit a pretty woman. He speaks French, English, Latin and a little Italian; he plays well on the lute and harpsichord, and can sing a piece of music as soon as he sees the page. He draws a bow with greater strength than any man in England and jousts marvellously.

Henry aged 22, enjoying himself with Queen Catherine at their palace at Greenwich:

It was the twelfth day of the Christmas feast, and during the evening a mountain pulled by four madmen rolled into the hall! It was called the Rich Mount, and was covered in silken flowers. All over it there were twigs of broom with stems of satin and flowers made of gold.

On top, around a flaming torch, sat the King and five others in coats and hats of crimson velvet embroidered and studded all over with gold.

The madmen brought the mountain to the Queen, where the King and the others leapt down and danced. After this the mountain suddenly opened and out came six ladies in coats and hats made of embroidered satin and wool. They danced alone; and they danced with the lords of the mountain. Finally they popped back into the mountain. The madmen towed it away again, and the King and the Queen sat down for the feast.

Henry as a young man

Read the descriptions of Henry as a teenager and the Christmas feast when he was 22.

1. How was Henry different from a modern teenager? There are several clues.
2. How do you think the mountain used at the Christmas feast was made?
3. Do you think the "madmen" were really mad? Why?
4. Henry had a habit of spending too much on his court (his palaces, family, advisers and servants). How can you tell that he spent a lot on his Christmas festivities?
5. Apart from spending a lot, what sort of person does Henry seem to have been when he was 22? (You may have several things to say.)
6. Draw or paint a picture of Henry's Christmas celebrations.

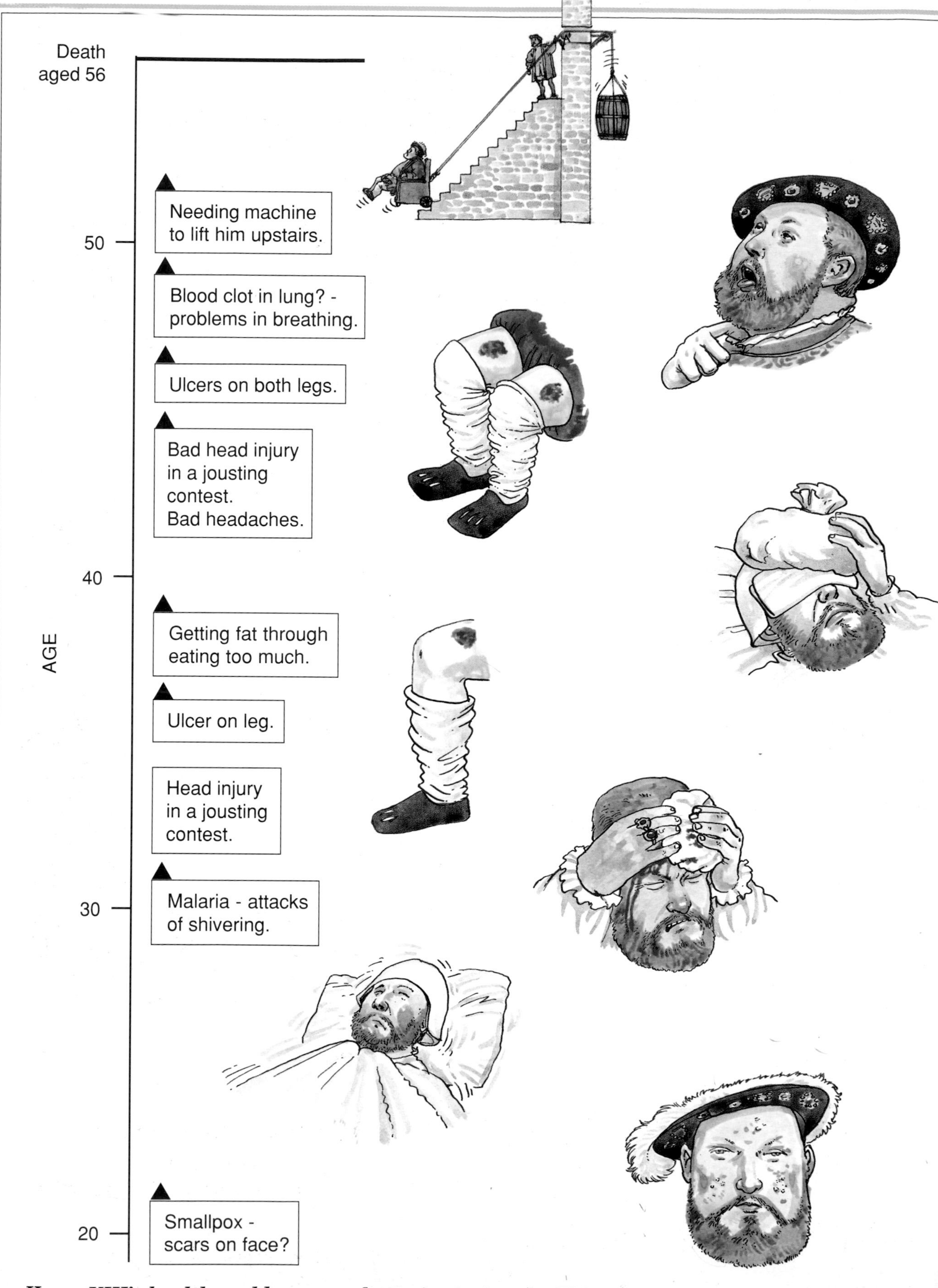

Henry VIII's health problems are shown in the boxes. This sign ▲ means that he was affected for the rest of his life. Do people in Britain have the same health problems nowadays?

Here are some more things people said about Henry:

Henry aged about 30:

His Majesty is very handsome and very well built. He has got a beard that looks like gold. He is good at music, an excellent horseman and clever with words. He has prayers three times a day when he hunts and five times a day when he stays at home.

Children at St. Matthew's Junior School, Luton completing a Henry VIII jigsaw puzzle.

A profile of Henry VIII

Look at the pictures of Henry in this chapter.

1. How old do you think he is in each picture?
2. What did each artist seem to think of Henry?
3. How do the eyes and other features make you feel?
4. Henry had scars on his face, but the pictures do not show them. Why do you think the artists left them out? Do you think they had to leave them out? Why?

Henry as "a sad, crippled, fat old man".

A man to remember

Look at the photograph of children doing a jigsaw puzzle.

1. Why do you think people still find Henry so interesting today?
2. Write a poem to describe Henry.

A fine new building of brick and timber, with water in pipes.

7. Tudor and Stuart Mansions

Hampton Court, near London, belonged to Cardinal Wolsey, who was Henry VIII's most important adviser. Wolsey helped Henry to destroy the monasteries, and he used some of their wealth to build Hampton Court. Other people also had fine country houses. Their houses were not as grand as Wolsey's, but compared with country cottages they must have seemed like palaces.

How many rooms do you think there are in this Tudor mansion?

Tudor and Stuart mansions were usually built of stone, so it was safe to have blazing fires against the walls. The houses had proper fireplaces, with chimneys to take the smoke away.

What would have been burnt in this large Tudor fireplace?

Hampton Court from the air.

Owners showed off their wealth by having glass in their windows. Glass was very scarce at first and they had to make do with small windows full of tiny panes. They sometimes made up for the shortage of glass by having windows with fancy shapes. Some looked like the "rose" windows in cathedrals. As glass became more plentiful, the owners used as much as they could.

How has the design of this window helped to save glass?

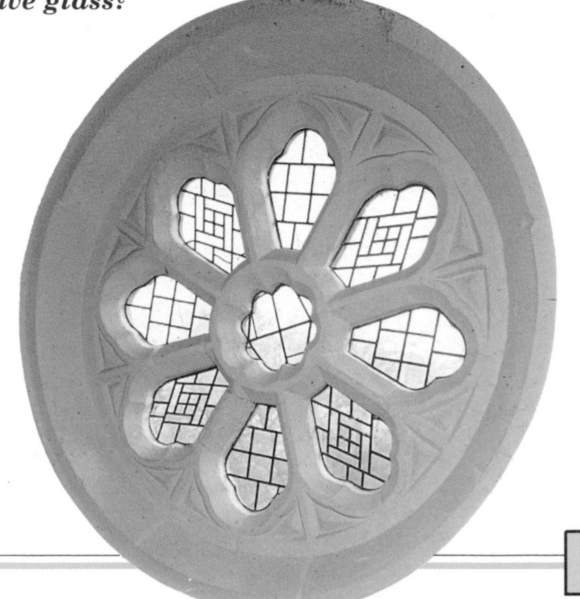

Dressing up in Tudor clothes and a hat. Tudor children had toys like the one the man is holding. How do you think they worked?

Keeping warm

Read all the information given in this chapter.

1. Owners of mansions used to have their dining tables and chairs on a low platform. Discuss some possible reasons for this.

Decorated windows

Look at the photographs of rose windows in this book.

1. Pretend you are a glass-maker in Tudor times. A wealthy family wants you to make coloured windows for their new mansion. Draw and colour the designs you will follow.

The Church was like a weather vane, changing with each new king or queen.

8. Church, King and Queen

The Church had always claimed that what it taught and did was based on the Bible. Now, in the 16th century, many churches got their own printed Bibles, and priests and scholars began to point out mistakes which the Church had made. Old teachings and habits disappeared, and services were simplified. These changes are called the Reformation.

In England the Reformation began when Henry VIII became head of the Church instead of the Pope. When Henry died in 1547 his son became King Edward VI, and Parliament made him head of the Church in Henry's place. He was only nine so other people ran the country for him, and they carried on with the Reformation:

- Priests had never been allowed to marry; now they could do so.
- Churches were stripped of statues and finery; everything had to be plain and simple.
- A simplified prayer book had to be used for all services. It was in English instead of the old language, Latin.
- Ordinary tables had to be used instead of altars.

Edward VI and his council (advisors).

A changing church

Read about the changes happening with the Reformation.

1. Copy out the following passage and complete the missing words:
   Scholars and scientists spread their ideas in p_____books. They did not always agree with the C_____or its leader, the P _____ , who lived in R _____.
   The R _____ ended the Pope's control of the Church in northern Europe. People who agreed with the Reformation are called P____ ; others are known as R______C______ .

Churches that changed at the Reformation are usually known as Protestant churches. Most of the people in England and northern Europe became Protestants, and they started calling the Pope's church the Roman Catholic Church.

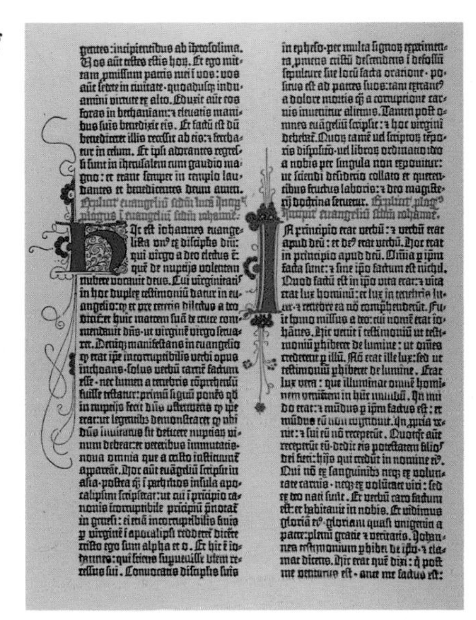

New printing machines allowed copies of the Bible to reach churches all over northern Europe.

Some people in northern Europe stuck to the Catholic faith. This led to serious trouble in Tudor and Stuart England. The worst trouble came when Edward VI died in his teens and Mary became queen. Mary's mother, Catherine of Aragon, came from Spain, which was fiercely Roman Catholic. Mary stuck to the Catholic

In Mary's reign several Protestant bishops were burned to death at the stake.

faith, and she undid everything Henry and Edward VI had done to the Church in England:

- Married priests lost their jobs.
- Altars and statues were put back in churches.
- Services had to be in Latin, and all the old beliefs were restored.
- The Pope was head of the Church again.

Queen Mary and Queen Elizabeth

Look at this page again.

1. Look at the portrait of Mary. What do you think the artist was trying to say about her?
2. Mary is sometimes called Bloody Mary. What does this suggest about the way she treated Protestants?
3. Which country might Elizabeth have feared? Why do you think so?

Elizabeth, who followed Mary, brought back Protestant worship but she let Roman Catholics worship in their own way at home.

Mary (sometimes called Mary Tudor).

A good May-game with giants, hobby-horses, drums, gongs, morris dancers and minstrels.

9. Fun and Games

A folding backgammon board recovered from a Tudor ship, "The Mary Rose".

The Tudors and Stuarts relaxed in many different ways. They enjoyed board games like backgammon and chess, and gambling games with cards and dice. Henry VIII lost most of his games and a great deal of money! The rich played tennis, but no one else could afford the special indoor courts that were used.

Many people played an outdoor game called "prison bars" or "prison base". They formed two teams and each team stood on its own patch of ground. When anyone tried to leave his patch the other team chased him and tried to take him prisoner. Girls and women did not play rough, lively games like this, but kings and princes joined in at court. (When Edward VI won the game he noted it down in his diary!)

Archery became a popular outdoor sport for both the rich and poor. The targets set up in a field were called butts. (We still use the word when we say that someone is the butt or target of an unkind joke. The word "butt" is also used in the names of some roads or districts.)

What differences can you see between Tudor tennis and the tennis most people play today?

Games

Read the description of games played in Tudor and Stuart days.

1. One way to learn about the past is to study the way things are today. Do you know a game like "prison bars"? What do you call it?
2. Men *had* to practise with bows and arrows. Why do you think this was important?
3. Is there a road or a district near you with "butt" in its name? What might youths and men have done there in Tudor times?

These Tudor archers are using crossbows.

Village youths played a very rough ball game: they formed two teams; then they fought their way across the countryside, with each team trying to get the ball to a different place - an inn, perhaps.

A Tudor writer called Sir Thomas Elyot wrote about the players' injuries:

Sometimes their necks are broken, sometimes their backs, sometimes their legs, sometimes their arms ... (The game) is nothing but beastly fury and extreme violence.

The rich had bloodthirsty sports too. While the poor shot at targets, the rich went hunting. There were royal forests that were full of deer and other game. Hunting was often followed by feasting.

Other violent games included fighting with sticks, boxing and wrestling. Rich people also enjoyed sword fights and jousting. In jousting contests, men in armour tried to knock each other off their horses with lances. The danger of death and injury must have increased the excitement. There was a special sort of jousting called quintain jousting. The riders aimed their lances at targets instead of each other, but they still risked being knocked off their horses. Quintain jousting did not require armour so anyone with a horse could try it.

Dreadful sports

Read Thomas Elyot's description of a ball game and the descriptions of other violent games.

1. Elyot said that the ball game should be banned, but this did not happen. It has developed into two modern games. Can you think what they are?
2. Some wrestlers wore hard shoes. Try to think of a reason for this.
3. Explain how quintain jousting worked. (The picture will help you.) Would you be good at it? Why do you think so?

Lances were used to turn the target in quintain jousting. What was this target made to look like?

Stocks, where people were locked as a punishment. (You could draw a picture of someone in them.)

Cockpits were places where people watched cockerels or other birds tearing each other to pieces.

Some Tudors and Stuarts liked to watch people and animals suffering. Crowds gathered to see criminals being hung or whipped, and they jeered at people who were in the stocks.

Someone living in Stuart times wrote:

In London there were two bear gardens with bears, bulls and other beasts. These animals were baited (tormented by savage dogs) in a plot of ground fenced in for the audience to stand safe.

For and against

Think about the entertainments described in this chapter.

1. Make a poster to advertise one of the shows.
   OR
2. Write a letter to the king or queen calling for the show to be banned.

Bears were trained to dance, and showmen took them around the country.

People could enjoy themselves and learn Bible stories at the same time. They did this by watching the stories being performed as plays in the open air. The actors were men from local guilds, which were rather like modern trade unions. They earned their living in all sorts of ways, but they were also paid a fee for their acting. The favourite date for the plays was Corpus Christi Day, a holy day in June, when the weather was warm and the days were long.

Each guild performed a different play from the Bible. A horse-drawn wagon covered in scenery was used as a stage. When the play ended, the wagon was towed away and the next set of actors rolled into position. If the town was large enough, the plays were performed at several sites. As soon as they finished in one place, the actors moved on to the next.

A modern artist's impression of a Bible story being acted on the back of a huge wagon. In Tudor and Stuart times men and boys played women's parts.

How are the guests enjoying themselves at this banquet?

Masques were sometimes performed in mansions and palaces. "Masque" is an old way of spelling "mask", and some or all of the people wore masks. There was acting, singing, dancing and feasting.

Describe the masks these people are wearing.

... can this cockpit hold
The vasty fields of France? or may we cram
Within this wooden O the very casques (helmets)
That did affright the air at Agincourt?

10. Theatres

Until Elizabeth came to the throne there were no theatres. Small groups of actors travelled from town to town and performed in the courtyards of inns. People who were staying at the inn could watch free of charge from their windows and balconies. Other people paid to come into the courtyard.

This inn still has the balconies where people watched plays.

The theatres built in Elizabeth's reign had balconies round an open space, rather like inns. Wealthy people paid to stand or sit on the balconies; the poorer people paid less and they stood in the open space around the stage.

We know about the buildings in various ways. We know about them from the **things people wrote**.

- The greatest playwright in Elizabeth's time was William Shakespeare. The lines above come from one of his plays. What do you think he meant by calling the theatre a "wooden O"?
- Someone described a fire at a theatre in 1613. He said it began when a cannon was fired as part of a play. The audience managed to get out safely, but someone had to have ale thrown over his burning breeches to put them out.

Some of Shakespeare's plays were performed at this theatre in London. When do you think the flag was raised?

William Shakespeare.

Excavating the Rose Theatre.

We know about them from **drawings people did at the time** and from **clues in the ground**.

- In 1989 archacologists found the remains of the Rose Theatre, where some of Shakespeare's plays were performed. The floor was made of soil and cinders, and it also had lots of nutshells in it. It was very hard but something had damaged it in front of the stage. The archaeologists had to try and work out how this had happened. In the end they decided that the stage must have had a roof, and the damage was caused by rainwater running off it on to the ground.

The stage included a balcony. There is a "balcony scene" in Shakespeare's *Romeo and Juliet*. Romeo is supposed to be calling from the street to Juliet's bedroom, so he uses the stage and Juliet - played by a man - uses the balcony.

Musicians also used the balcony above the stage, playing trumpet calls and other music to go with the action. The performers had costumes but not much scenery. Sometimes they put a wall, a bush or a throne on the stage, but the audience had to use a lot of imagination!

Watching a play

Using information given in this chapter, imagine the scene in a theatre during Queen Elizabeth's reign.

1. What refreshments would the audience be eating and drinking?
2. There were trapdoors in the floor of the stage. Suggest when the actors might use them.
3. The lines at the start of this chapter mention a famous battlefield (Agincourt). Why will the audience have to use their imagination?
4. Discuss why *theatres* did not have a roof. What advantages and disadvantages did this have?
5. Imagine that *you* are at the Rose Theatre. Draw or describe what you can see.

The balcony was always needed in Shakespeare's Romeo and Juliet.

Their fleet consists of mighty ships and great strength ... yet we pluck their feathers little by little.

11. The Spanish Armada

In Elizabeth's reign, Spain was the world's most powerful Roman Catholic country. Spain ruled Portugal, the Netherlands and much of North and South America. Spanish sailors had helped to discover America, and their ships were now coming home full of gold and other treasure.

Encouraged by the Pope, the Spaniards decided to conquer Queen Elizabeth's England. They were tired of English pirates looting Spanish treasure ships and they disliked the fact that the English had started to claim parts of North and South America for themselves.

An Englishman called Sir Francis Drake had just sailed round the world, attacking the Spaniards on land and at sea; he was one of the first men to make such a voyage. Another Englishman, Sir Walter Raleigh, had recently started a colony in Virginia, North America. Tobacco grew in the area, and Raleigh brought the habit of smoking to England.

Raleigh's colony soon disappeared, and some people think the native Americans killed the settlers. However, at the time of the Armada in 1588, the growth of British colonies worried the Spaniards a lot. (Under the Stuarts, the British started colonies in many parts of North America and they turned Virginia into a very important growing area.)

A famous picture of Queen Elizabeth. What can you see in the panels behind her?

Taking sides

Look again at the start of this page.

1. Why do you think the Pope encouraged the Spaniards to attack England?

A fleet at sea.

An hourglass used for telling the time at sea.

Just before the Armada sailed, the Spanish King, Philip II, gave his captains some important advice:

The English will want to fight at a distance, because of their advantage with cannons - which they fire low to sink their enemies' ships - and because of the many artificial fires which they will have. The aim of our men must be to get close to the English and grapple with them.

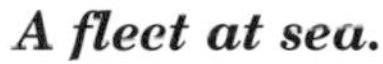

Frightening details

The English found out details of the Spanish fleet from a booklet which the Spaniards produced before the fleet sailed.

1. Countries usually keep their war plans secret. Why do you think the Spaniards produced the booklet? *(Clue:* How do you think the English felt when they heard about torture instruments on the Spanish ships?*)*
2. Do you think we can trust all the facts and figures in the booklets? Why?
3. What do you think King Philip meant by "artificial fires"? How might fire be used against the Spanish ships?

An English writer called Richard Hakluyt described the Spanish fleet.

The ships had everything needed on board such as carts, wheels, wagons, etc. They also had spades, mattocks, pickaxes and baskets so that settlers could quickly get to work. They had mules, horses and everything else a land army needed. They were so well stocked with biscuits that for half a year each man in the fleet could have half a quintal (25 kilos) every month ...

They had 147,000 casks of wine - again enough for half a year's voyage. They had butter and cheese, besides fish, rice, beans, peas, oil, vinegar, etc.

On top of that they had 12,000 casks of fresh water and ... candles, lanterns, lamps, sails, hemp, ox-hides and lead to stop up holes.

The Armada was reckoned by the King himself to contain 32,000 persons.

The Spaniards also had racks, thumbscrews, whips and knives.

After saying prayers and putting holy signs on their ships the Spaniards sailed for England in May 1588.

Things soon started going wrong for the Spaniards.

ORDERS,
Set dovvne by th
Duke of Medina, Lord general
of the Kings Fleet, to be obserued in
the voyage toward England.

Translated out of Spanish into English by T.P.

Imprinted at London by Thomas Orwin for Th
mas Gilbert, dwelling in Fleetstreete neere to
the signe of the Castle. 1588.

The first page of the booklet in which the Spaniards described their fleet.

According to an English sailor, the Spaniards anchored near Calais and the English took eight very old ships and sent them:

... towards the Spanish fleet at two in the morning, with the wind and tide to carry them. When they had gone a good distance they were set on fire and left to float right to the King of Spain's navy. This fire in the dead of night put the Spaniards in such a panic that they cut the cables their anchors were joined to, raised their sails and took to the open sea in confusion.

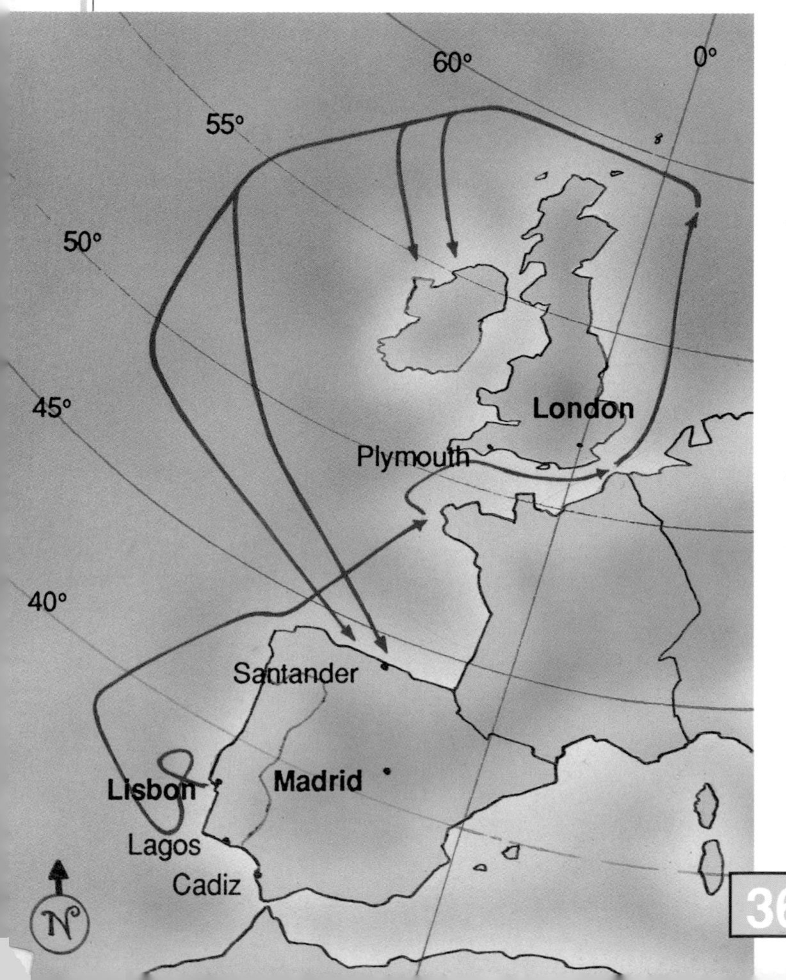

The journey made by the Spanish Armada. You can see where some ships ran aground.

Later, the wind gave the Spaniards new problems. Blowing from the south, it pushed the Armada northwards into the North Sea. With the English behind them they fled up the coast of northern England. They carried on northwards, even when the English turned back. They hoped to get back to Spain by going round Scotland and Ireland. A lot of the ships were wrecked but half got back to Spain.

Some of the Spaniards had been at sea for nearly a year. There had been little fresh food on the ships and many of the Spaniards had died because of their bad diet. Others had bleeding gums and diarrhoea. The English reached home sooner but many of them were ill too.

When the Spanish fleet was threatening England, most of Elizabeth's troops were at Tilbury, ready to deal with the Spaniards if they tried to land. Here is part of the speech she gave them:

I have come in the heat of battle to live or die amongst you all; to lay down for my God, for my kingdom and for my people my honour and my blood, even in this dust.

I know that I have the body of a weak and feeble woman but I have the heart and stomach of a king, and a king of England too, and I think it foul that Spain or any prince of Europe should dare to invade the borders of my realm. I know you have deserved rewards and crowns; and I promise you on the word of a prince that they shall be paid to you.

We shall have a famous victory over these enemies of my God, my kingdom and my people.

A rousing speech

Read the speech given by Queen Elizabeth and look at the map.

1. Where would you have stationed most of your troops at this dangerous time if you had been the king or queen? (You could use an atlas to see if Elizabeth's choice was similar.)
2. Some people think that Elizabeth's speech - especially the first part - was rather dishonest. What do you think?
3. Leaders often give stirring speeches in wartime. Why do they take the trouble to do this?
4. What do you think hungry sailors would have thought of Queen Elizabeth's speech?
5. Study the portrait of Queen Elizabeth on page 34. What does it say about the Armada?

An account of a battle

Pretend that you are a sailor or priest on one of the Spanish ships.

1. Write about one or two of the most exciting or unpleasant days you spent at sea.

Queen Elizabeth giving the speech to her troops.

The Welsh had the labour and strangers had the profit.

Wool was prepared for spinning using a carding brush, like a giant comb.

12. Life in Wales

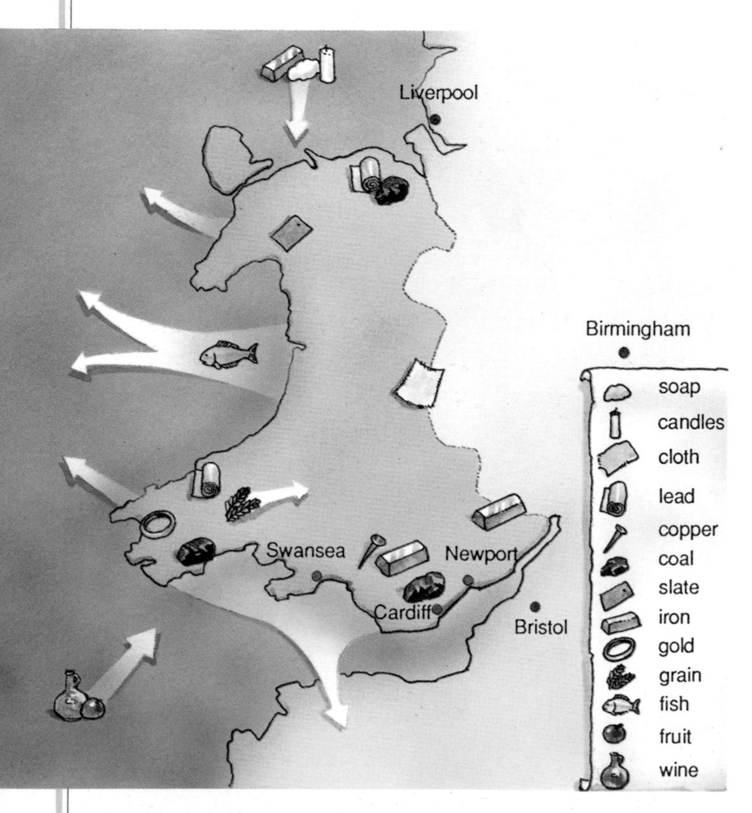

Did the Welsh receive many goods in return for the things they supplied?

Wales had once been a separate country but the English had conquered it, treating it like a part of England. They expected the Welsh to obey English laws and they let them choose their own members of Parliament. As in England, they closed down the monasteries, ended obedience to the Pope and translated the Latin Bible into people's everyday language (in this case Welsh).

Many of the people were sheep farmers living high up in the hills. They turned the sheep's wool into clothes for themselves and they also sold cloth to English merchants. Sometimes the English treated the Welsh unfairly, making them sell their cloth to English merchants at very low prices.

Would you have wanted to work like these men?

The Welsh also sold coal, metal and stone mined from their mountains. Like farming, mining was usually done by families. Sometimes the miners found the coal and rock at the surface, but usually they had to dig pits. There might be two men chipping away at the coal or rock with axes and putting the pieces into a barrel. Other men then had to haul the full barrel out of the pit.

Transporting coal and other goods was difficult because of the mountains. Wealthy people burnt coal to keep warm, and they bought it from mines very near their homes. Stone and coal from mines near the sea was carried by boat, and Wales had some very busy ports.

Working in Wales

Read the information in this chapter.

1. "The Welsh had the labour and strangers had the profit." What do you think people meant by this?
2. The drawings show Welsh people working hard. What are they doing?
3. How was Wales different from England? How was it similar?

The English feared that invaders from Scotland, Ireland or Spain would land in Wales. Wales had many lonely bays all round the coast where invaders could land in secret, and mountains where they could gather their forces. They might get some of the Welsh on their side and then attack England. To control the Welsh and to deal with invaders the English built large castles in Wales.

From Caernarfon Castle, the English watched for enemies who might attack Wales from the sea.

Look for the Parliament House which Catesby planned to blow up.

... they shall receive a terrible blow.

13. The Gunpowder Plot

Queen Elizabeth did not have any children, so when she died King James of Scotland agreed to be king of England too. James was a Protestant like Elizabeth, but unlike Elizabeth, he began to treat Roman Catholics harshly.

In 1605 some angry Roman Catholics led by Robert Catesby plotted to blow up King James and the rest of his Parliament and then lead a rising in the Midlands. They wanted to replace James with a Roman Catholic. The date they chose was 5th November, when their victims would all be in Parliament.

At the end of October a man called Lord Mounteagle went to one of the King's advisers. He said that a stranger had just brought him this mysterious, unsigned letter:

My lord, I would advise you to shift your attendance at this Parliament ... Retire yourself into your country where you may expect the event in safety, for though there be no appearance of any stir yet I say they shall receive a terrible blow this Parliament.

The King and his advisers arranged for guards to go to Parliament at midnight on the 4th November. One of the guards described what the man in charge of them did:

Finding a man (called Guy Fawkes) standing outside the door with his clothes and boots on at so dead a time of the night he arrested him; then we went outside to search the house. (Behind some logs and coal) he found one of the small barrels of gunpowder and afterwards all the rest to the number of 36 great and small; and thereafter found three matches and all other instruments fit for blowing up the powder ready upon him.

One plotter is missing from the picture. Who is it?

The murder plan had failed, but most of the plotters left London on horseback and started their rising. Only Fawkes and a plotter called Francis Tresham remained in London.

The rising failed because few people joined it. The king's officials found some of the plotters and shot them dead, but they arrested most of the leaders. They took them to London where they were tried and hanged.

Tresham (who was Mounteagle's brother-in-law) was treated differently. The king's men did not arrest him at first but later they put him in prison without giving any clear reason. He fell ill, died and was quickly "tumbled into a hole". One doctor said that he had been poisoned, but no one is sure what really happened.

Solving some mysteries

Think about the Gunpowder Plot and how it was foiled.

1. Who might have written the unsigned letter? Why do you think so?
2. Guy Fawkes was arrested only just in time. Do you think he could have been arrested sooner? Why do you think so?
3. Why might the king's advisers have chosen to wait until the night of 4th November?
4. Discuss Francis Tresham and his part in the Gunpowder Plot. Then write a piece called *Francis Tresham - the Mystery Solved.*
   OR
   Choose someone who is mentioned in this chapter and write down questions to ask them about the Plot. Swap your list with a friend and answer each other's questions.

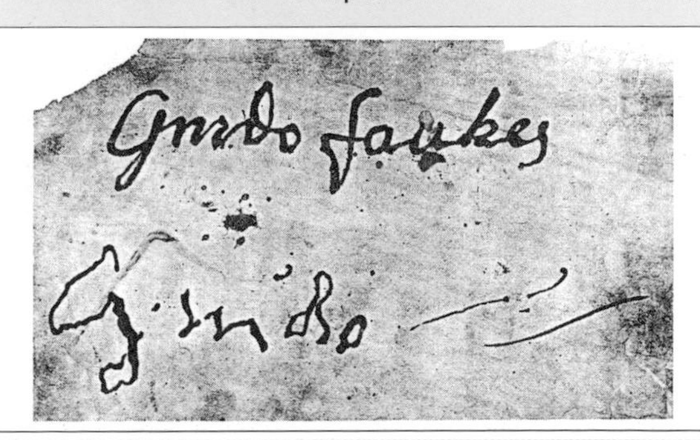

Guy Fawkes's signature changed in the last few weeks of his life. How do you think he was being treated?

Kings are justly called gods: they make and unmake their subjects; they have power of raising and casting down; of life and of death.

14. James the Author

This carving at Oxford shows James giving books to two people. One stands for Oxford University and the other stands for James's future fame. Which is which?

King James liked reading, watching plays and writing books. Some of his books were printed and sold, and they show us the sort of person he was. For example, his book *Demonology* shows that he was frightened of being cursed or having a spell put on him. James was afraid of other things too - he wore padded clothes in case his enemies tried to use daggers instead of magic.

Some of the things James wrote helped to make new enemies for him. For example, in *Basilikon Doron* he wrote about how special kings were. He said that a king was "a little god" who should always be obeyed without question. This attitude upset Parliament - the members felt they had a right to challenge James's decisions.

One of James's most famous books is his *Counterblast to Tobacco*. A counterblast is an angry reply, and James was arguing back at people who said there was nothing wrong with smoking.

We cannot be content unless we imitate everything that our fellows do ... (We are) like apes, counterfeiting (copying) others, to our own destruction.

Shakespeare wrote his weird and frightening play* Macbeth *with James in mind. James must have felt great pleasure - and fear - when Shakespeare's actors performed it at court.

James was sorry for wives whose husbands stank of smoke. He said they sometimes took up smoking to make themselves smell as bad as their husbands. This was their only way of getting used to the stink.

Although he was quite a nervous person, James liked the dangers and thrills of hunting and he wanted people to enjoy themselves properly. He did not like the people who said that no one should have any fun on a Sunday. In his *Book of Sports* he said that dancing, games and feasts should all be allowed, provided people had been to church first.

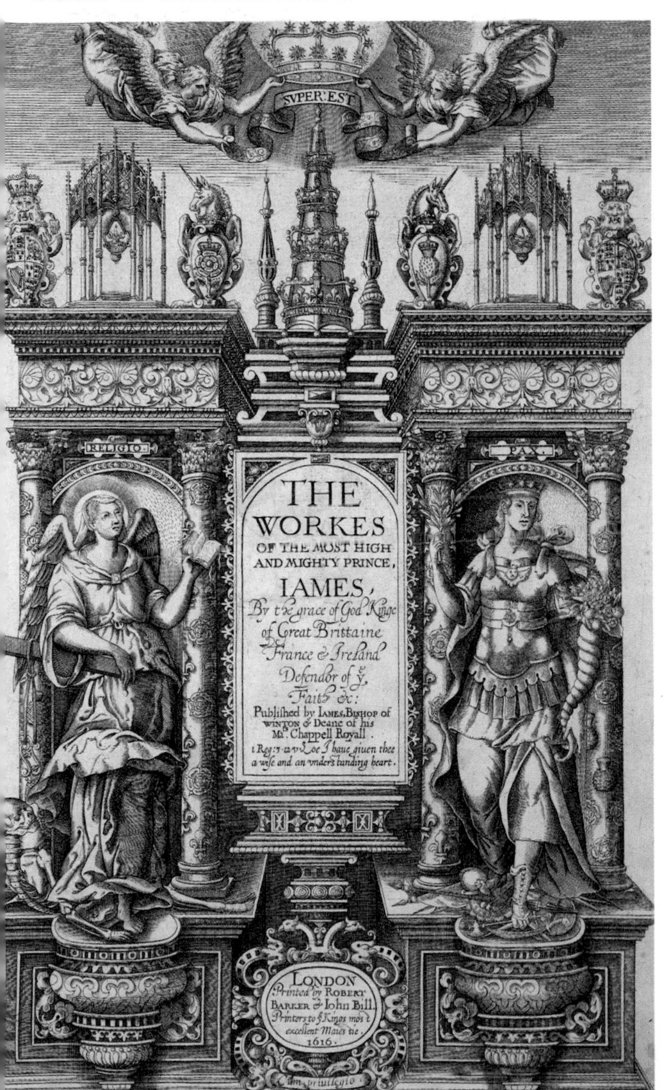
SVPER EST

RELIGIO

PAX

THE WORKES OF THE MOST HIGH AND MIGHTY PRINCE, IAMES,

By the grace of God Kinge of Great Brittaine France & Ireland Defendor of ye Faith &c:

Published by IAMES, BISHOP of WINTON & Deane of his Ma.ts Chappell Royall.

LONDON Printed by ROBERT BARKER & Iohn Bill, Printers to ye Kings most excellent Maiestie 1616.

***The opening page from* The Workes of the Most High and Mighty Prince, James.**

Educating the prince

When he was young, James had lessons at home. Pretend that you are his tutor (teacher).

1. Write a report on his work and his character. Use your imagination, but also think about what he was like as a man. There are clues in this chapter.

At the start of his reign, James asked a team of scholars to make a new translation of the Bible. The old translations had been in use for 100 years since the time of the Tudors. They contained mistakes, and the old-fashioned language made them hard to understand.

The new version came out in 1611, and most people felt that the language was clear and beautiful. The *King James' Bible* has been reprinted and used ever since, though many newer translations exist.

Some people, known as Puritans, wanted to make church services simpler than ever. They lived strict lives, working hard, avoiding luxuries and dressing plainly. James disliked the Puritans' religious beliefs and he treated them harshly.

Speeches and books

Read about the books King James wrote.

1. The words at the start of this chapter come from one of James's speeches to Parliament. What do you think the Members thought of it?
2. Which of James's books contained the same ideas as his speech?
3. What do you think Puritans thought of *The Book of Sports*?

A troop of devils, a heap of scum and rubbish and garbage, a bloody and butcherly class of men.

15. Charles I and Parliament

Charles I.

At the start of 1642:

The King went to Parliament with a company of cavaliers (horsemen) with swords and pistols to have five of the Members charged with high treason. But the King was not so secret or speedy in his action and the Members had notice of it before his coming in ... and so the King and his company laid hands on none, but went their ways.

James died in 1625 and his son Charles took his place as king. Like his father, Charles felt that a king was "a little god". He asked Parliament to approve new taxes and when the Members refused he sent them home and collected the money anyway.

In 1629 Charles began to rule without Parliament, but by 1640 he was desperate for money. He called the Members of Parliament together, sent them home when they would not agree to extra taxes and then called them back. Charles was making himself look foolish, and not like "a little god" at all! The Members felt it was time to show their strength and they made a new law that stopped Charles trying to send them home.

People were angered that Charles had ignored the Members' rights to meet in safety, and it seemed that there might be a war between Charles and Parliament.

The danger of war increased when the Irish began to throw English settlers out of their country. Charles and Parliament agreed to send an army, but Parliament insisted on choosing the commanders and controlling the bands of men trained to fight in time of war.

Some of the King's Supporters felt that Parliament's control of the fighters was dangerous. One man spoke of:

A preparation of arms against the King under shadow (appearance) of loyalty.

Danger ahead

Read about the incidents which were happening in Parliament between 1625 and 1642.

1. Charles once said, "I see that all the birds are flown". When do you think he made this remark?
2. What did Parliament do that was dangerous for Charles? Why was it dangerous?

Look for the Roundheads and the Royalists in these battle pictures.

War between King and Parliament broke out in 1642. Oliver Cromwell was one of the men who led Parliament's forces. Most of them kept their hair cut short, so they were known as Roundheads. Charles's men were called Royalists or Cavaliers.

A war within a country is called a civil war. Sometimes neighbours - or members of a family - take different sides and this causes terrible bitterness. At the start of this chapter you can read what the Roundheads said about the Cavaliers.

Cromwell was a Puritan. This drawing gives a Puritan view of the Royalists.

Cruelties of war

Look at the drawing of the Battle, which appeared in about 1644.

1. What does it show?
2. Who do you think produced it? Why do you think they took this trouble?

16. Cromwell's Victory

Oliver Cromwell.

In the summer of 1645 the Roundheads won an important battle at Naseby in Northamptonshire. The Royalists never recovered their strength, and in May 1646 Charles surrendered. His only hope now was to use his pen and tongue as cunningly as he could.

Charles's enemies included Oliver Cromwell and his army, the Scots and many Members of Parliament. Charles talked to them separately, hoping to make them quarrel among themselves and perhaps get one group on his side. His plan nearly worked, and Cromwell's troops had to fight to keep order. Cromwell called Charles a "Man of Blood" for causing more trouble.

In December 1648 a band of soldiers went to Parliament and threw out Members who did not support Cromwell. Parliament then decided to put the king on trial.

Throughout his trial Charles argued that the court had no right to judge a king. Despite this, the court sentenced Charles to death. They called him "a tyrant, traitor, murderer and public enemy".

Charles's trial

Look at the pictures of the court.

1. In each picture pick out Charles.
2. What different ideas do the pictures give of the atmosphere at Charles's trial?
3. What would help you to find out more about the trial? (The men at the table and the things they are using should give you a clue.)

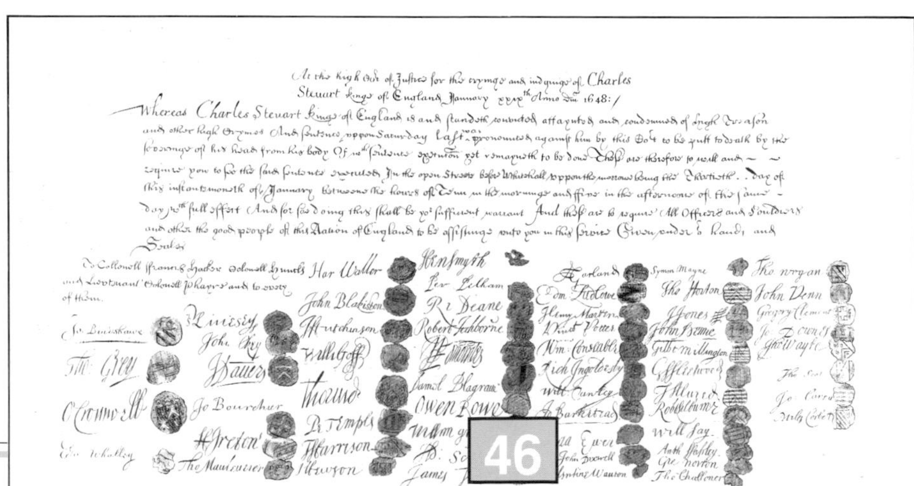
At the high Court of Justice for the tryinge and judginge of Charles Steuart Kinge of England January xxix Anno Dni 1648:/

Whereas Charles Steuart Kinge of England is and standeth convicted attaynted and condemned of High Treason and other high Crymes And sentence uppon Saturday last was pronounced against him by this Court to be putt to death by the severinge of his head from his body Of wch sentence execucon yet remayneth to be done These are therefore to will and require you to see the said sentence executed In the open Streete before Whitehall uppon the morrowe being the Thirtieth day of this instante moneth of January betweene the houres of Tenn in the morninge and Five in the afternoone of the same day wth full effect And for soe doing this shall be yor sufficient warrant And these are to require All Officers and Souldiers and other the good people of this Nation of England to be assistinge unto you in this service Given under our hands and Seales

To Collonell ffrancis Hacker Collonell Huncks and Leivtenant Collonell Phayre and to every of them.

The letter demanding Charles's death. How many people signed it?

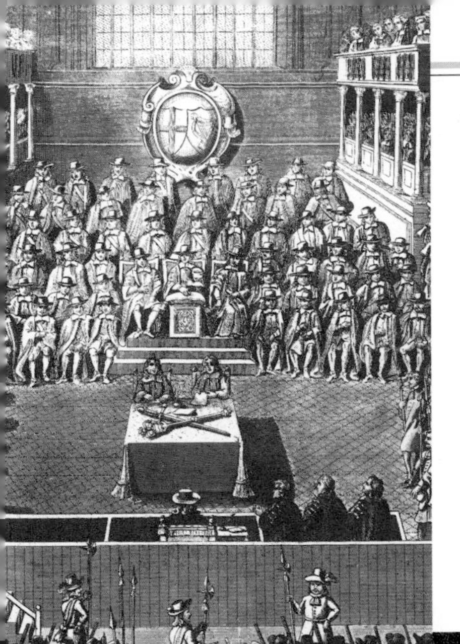

Drawings of Charles's trial.

The execution of Charles.

Cromwell was now the most important person in England, and he took the title of Lord Protector. When Parliament made him angry he closed it down and ruled by himself - just as Charles had done. Cromwell and his Puritan friends also closed all theatres and places of entertainment. Life was peaceful, dull and orderly.

Cromwell died in 1658 and his son Richard tried to take over as Lord Protector. He was such a weak ruler that some people called him Tumbledown Dick. With the country in chaos, Parliament invited Charles's son to become king and he agreed to do so. He is known as Charles II. The return to having a king is called the Restoration.

Acting out the trial

Use your imagination and evidence from this chapter.

1. Work with a partner. One of you should make up questions or accusations that Cromwell might have put to Charles. The other should answer them as Charles might have done.
2. Think about the things that happened under Charles and Cromwell. What lessons do you think people should have learned?

She sat there dead. She was "in a sick dress that stank mightily".

17. The Plague of 1665

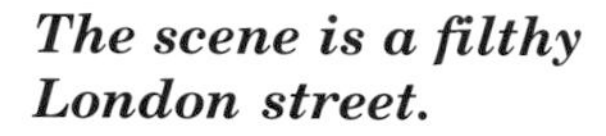

The scene is a filthy London street.

Look at the map of London on the opposite page. Smithfield, was the only large open space, but it was not a place where people could go and get fresh air. Farmers from all around London drove their cattle there for butchers to buy, so the area stank of dung and blood. Other parts of the city stank too. There were no proper toilets, and some people used a hole in the ground at the back of their houses; others used a chamber-pot and emptied the contents into the street. The filth often reached the streams and wells where people got their drinking water, so thousands of Londoners died each year from diarrhoea and sickness.

A crowded, unclean city

Look at the map of London in Stuart times.

1. Do you think the city was cramped or spacious?
2. The centre of London had a wall round three sides. Why do you think the wall was built? Why do you think there was no wall on the southern side?
3. The wall was built in Tudor times. Do you think the city got bigger or smaller after that? Why do you think so?

Upper storeys of houses often stuck out so that houses on opposite sides of an alley almost touched. Sunlight never reached the ground and rats and insects thrived in the gloomy, dirty conditions. These vermin spread diseases quickly. Men were paid to clean the streets, but often they only put the filth into London's river, the Thames. The river ebbs and flows with the tide, so the same lot of filth kept coming back and more was being added all the time.

People had fleas all over them. Fleas live on blood, and sometimes a flea sucked a rat's blood and then a human being's. This was very dangerous, since rats often had a disease called plague, and the fleas passed it on from the rats to the people.

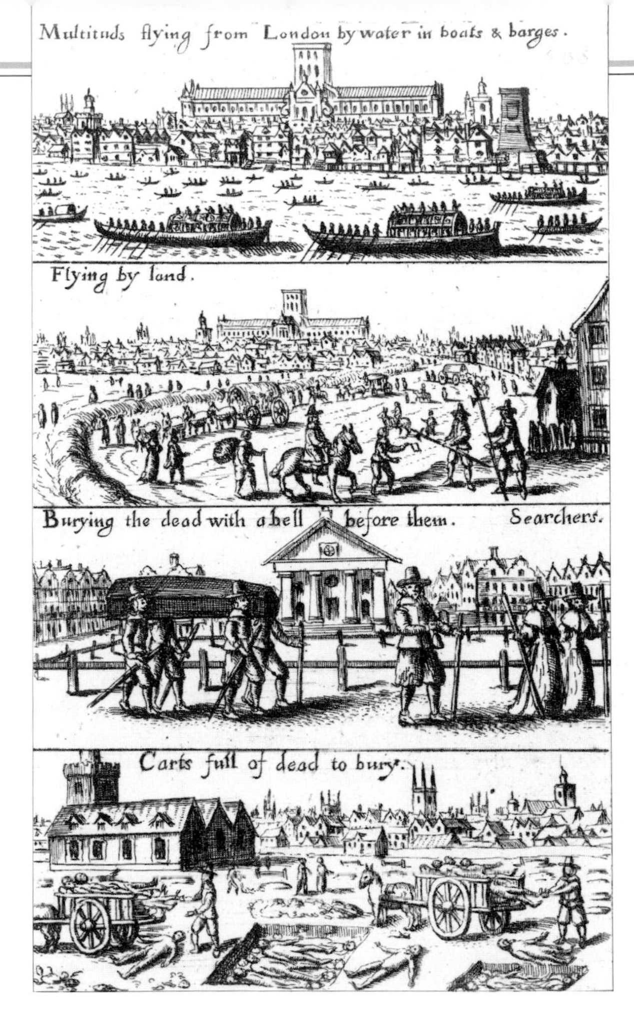

▲ ***Coping with the effects of the plague.***

▼ ***London at the time of the plague.***

In 1665 many Londoners started dying of plague. In early June a man called Samuel Pepys wrote in his diary:

This day I did in Drury Lane see two or three houses marked with a red cross upon the door and 'Lord have mercy upon us' written there.

Samuel Pepys has become famous because his diary gives a detailed picture of life in London during the reign of Charles II.

Few but the poor - who had nowhere to go - stayed in London. People fled to the countryside thinking that they would be safer there. Pepys remained in the city because of his work but he made his will and prepared to die. Each night he heard carts going though the streets to collect dead bodies. The poor were buried together in pits, but richer folk had proper graves.

Just outside London some youths saw a curtained coach in a lane. They popped their heads through the curtains to frighten the person inside, but they were the ones who got the fright - the woman was dead. She was "in a sick dress that stank mightily" and was being taken away to be buried.

The following week Pepys was riding in a coach when it suddenly stopped. The coachman staggered down and said he was sick and half blind. The plague was reaching everyone.

Pepys was lucky. He did not catch the plague, and he wrote in his diary:

I have never lived so merrily (or earned so much) as I have done this plague time.

Pages from Pepys' diary. He wrote it in code so that no one would discover his secrets, but since his death people have worked out what it says.

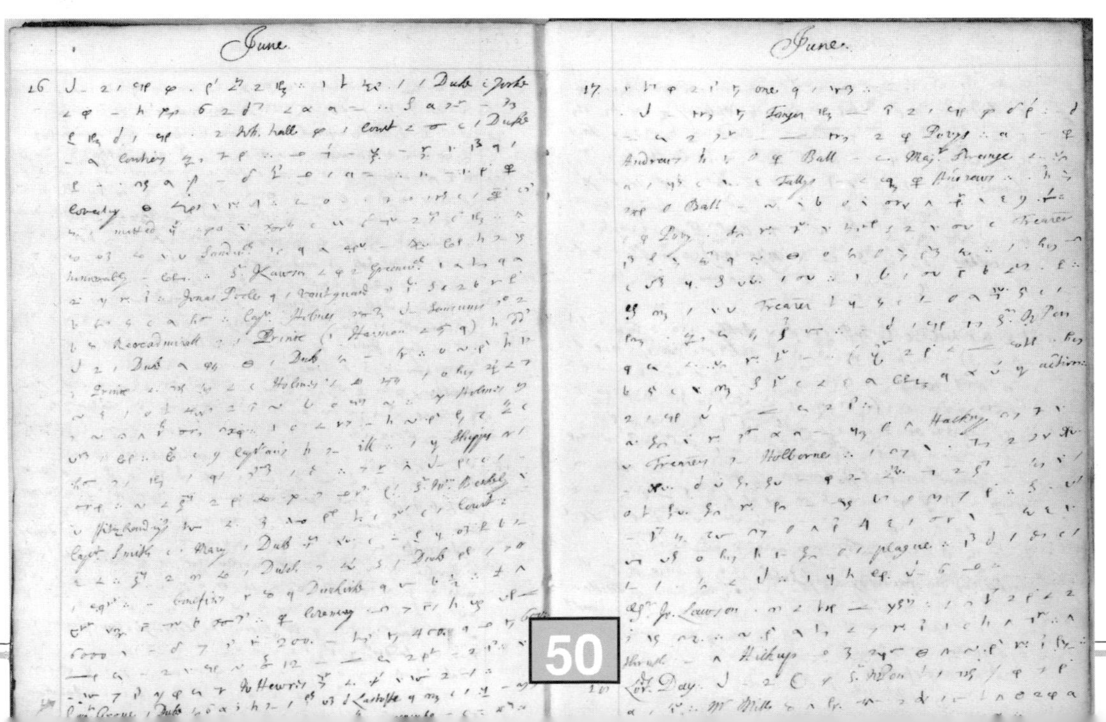

Stuart London

Read this chapter.

1. How do you think goods were transported round London? How did wealthy people travel?
2. Which forms of transport are better - modern ones or the ones that were used in Stuart times? Why do you think so?
3. Draw one of the scenes which Pepys saw in London.

Doctors believed these special clothes would help to protect them from the plague.

Back to the past

Suppose you could travel backwards in time.

1. What advice would you give to people in London to help them to make their lives more healthy? List the points and work with friends to design a poster.

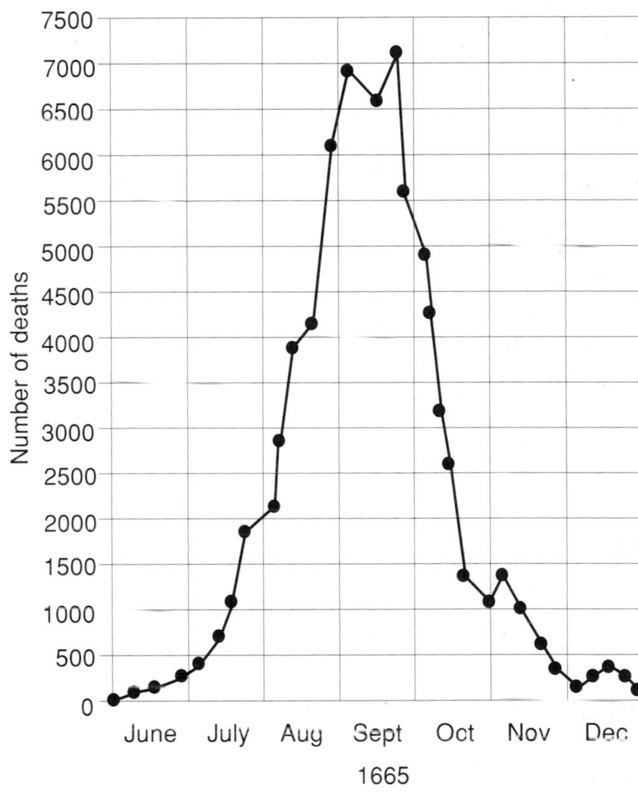

This graph shows how many Londoners died of plague each week.

The dreadful plague

Look at the picture of the doctor and study the chart.

1. Before going out, this doctor stuffed the "beak" of his gown with flowers. Why do you think he did this?
2. Which month was the plague worst?
3. What was the greatest number of people to die in a week?

The white area on this map shows the parts of London destroyed in the Great Fire.

Jane (the servant) called us about three in the morning to tell us of a great fire; I rose and went to the window ... I thought it far enough off and so went to bed again.

18. The Great Fire of London

The words above come from Pepys' diary. It was the summer of 1666 and the Great Fire of London had just begun. It had broken out in Pudding Lane, destroying all the bakers' shops. By morning Fish Street, too, had disappeared in smoke and flame. The houses had all been built of wood, with a coating of tar to stop the rain coming in. The tar was helping the wood to burn. Along the riverside people were hurling their furniture into boats, or even into the water itself.

Pepys described how pigeons flew too near the flames. Their wings got burnt and they fell to their death.

Pepys said that buildings were disappearing ...

... in a most horrid, malicious bloody flame and not like the flame of an ordinary fire. It made me weep to see it . The churches, houses all on fire and flaming at once; and a horrid noise the flames made and the crackling of houses at their ruin.

Pepys and his wife put chests of money in their cellar, and they buried bags of gold and boxes of papers in their garden. Pepys also buried paper, wine and cheese near his office.

The fire was creeping near to the Tower of London where the army stored its gunpowder. Officials were afraid that the heat would ignite the gunpowder. To stop this happening they blew up houses in nearby Tower Street to make a gap that the fire could not spread across.

At two o'clock the following morning, Pepys and his wife escaped by river. He returned the next day to see his house and the Tower still standing. The fire was dying down but hardly any of the city inside the walls had survived.

Activity in the fire

Follow the actions of people in the fire.

1. The fire reached the end of Pepys' road but Pepys' house and nearby office were not burnt down. What do you think they were built of?
2. Why do you think some people put their property in churches? Which famous church did the fire destroy?
3. Think about the things Pepys buried. What do they tell us about the sort of person Pepys was?

The newly-built streets were less crowded than before, and cleaner too. This helped to prevent fresh outbreaks of plague and London has never had one since.

A few years later a man called Sir John Reresby wrote:

The dreadful effects of the fire were not so strange as the rebuilding of this great city. By reason of the King's and Parliament's care and the great wealth of the city itself (it) was rebuilt most stately with brick (the greatest part being before nothing but planks and lime) in four or five years.

The Tower of London.

St. Paul's Cathedral as it is today. A famous architect, called Sir Christopher Wren, drew the plans for this magnificent building.

Nature and nature's laws lay hid in night; God said, "Let Newton be," and all was light.

19. Science in Stuart Times

Science and medicine made rapid progress in Stuart times. Until then, it was thought that blood went backwards and forwards in the body, changing direction with every heartbeat. A doctor called William Harvey proved that this was wrong.

William Harvey telling Charles I how the heart works.

He found valves (small flaps) in the blood pipes that let the blood go one way but not the other. After leaving the heart it can only get back by circulating all round the body.

Up to this time, few people ever saw a doctor, even if they were really ill. In towns there were herbalists - men and women who sold medicines made from plants. Towns also had barbers who cut hair, pulled out teeth and bled people (let out some of their blood in the hope of curing their illnesses).

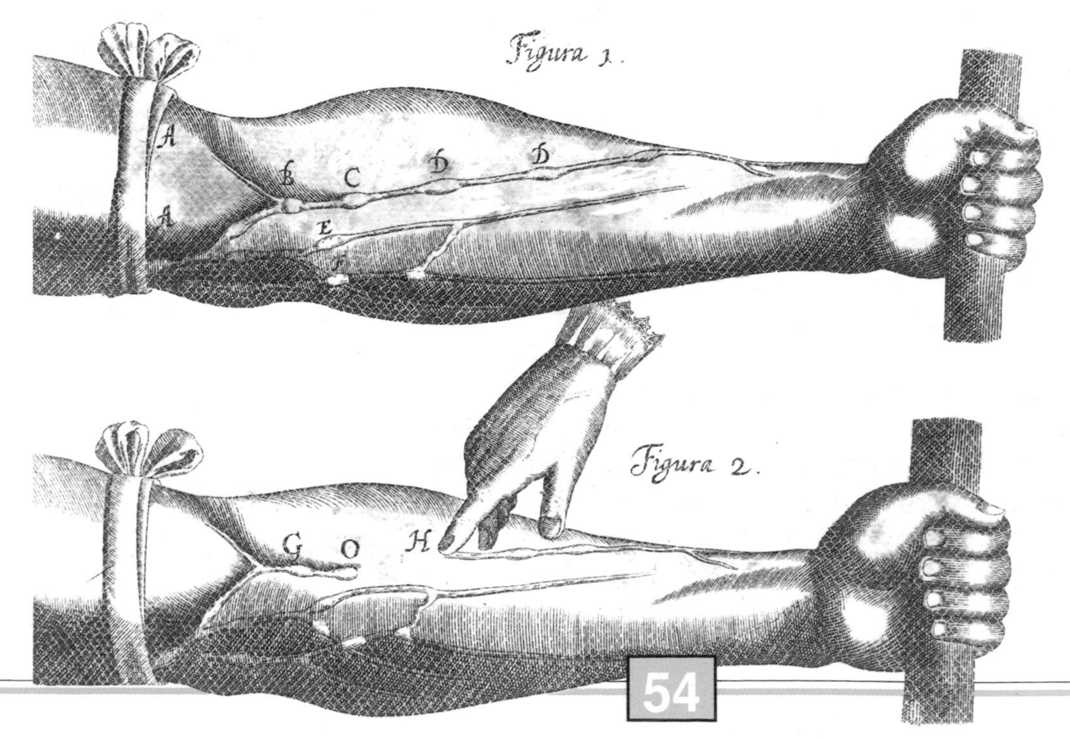

William Harvey did simple experiments to prove that there are valves in our veins. These drawings come from one of his books.

Hairdresser, doctor or dentist?

Look at the shop sign common in Tudor and Stuart times.

1. We sometimes see this sign today. What shops use it?
2. Think about what they used to do for their customers and find out what the sign is meant to show.

A Tudor shop.

In 1666, King Charles II helped a group of scientists to set up a new society. It was called the Royal Society for the Advancement of Science. The Royal Society still exists today and it aims to help scientists with their work.

Pepys, one of the Royal Society's earliest members, describes what he saw at one of its meetings:

... there was a pretty experiment of the blood of one dog let out into the body of another, while all his own ran out. The first died on the spot, and the other is very well and likely to do well. This may be of mighty use to men's health, for the mending of bad blood by the borrowing from a better body.

Newton found that a prism (wedge of glass), could split white light into all the colours of the rainbow.

The most famous scientist to live at this time was Isaac Newton. Light was one of the mysteries which Newton studied.

Newton also studied gravity - the mysterious way things pull on each other. Some people say that Newton began to think about gravity when he saw an apple fall from a tree and wondered if the earth had attracted (pulled) it down.

He began to think about the movement of huge things like planets, and he worked out their paths as they travel through space. He was helped by a new invention, the telescope, which had just arrived in England from Europe.

An early telescope.

Index